Native American
SIGN LANGUAGE

by Madeline Olsen • illustrated by Ben Carter

Troll

For Marisa—M.O.

Artist Ben Carter is of Comanche descent. His oil paintings and watercolors often focus on scenes of Western life. While he has lived most of his life in Texas, he pursued his advanced training at the Art Academy of Chicago and the Art Institute of Chicago.

Developed by Nancy Hall, Inc. Text copyright © 1998 by Nancy Hall, Inc. Illustrations copyright © 1998 by Ben Carter.
Published by Troll Communications L.L.C. All rights reserved. No part of this book may be reproduced or
utilized in any form or by any means, electronic or mechanical, including photocopying, recording,
or by any information storage and retrieval system, without written permission from
the publisher. Printed in the United States of America. ISBN 0-8167-4509-9.
10 9 8 7 6 5 4 3 2 1

Dear Reader,

I was very pleased when I was asked to review this book on sign language, a subject often overlooked in telling the history of our people.

The use of sign language by the Plains peoples for hunting and tracking has long since passed. However, it is still used today on many occasions to help emphasize and clarify the spoken word. I sometimes think about an experience I had out on the Pine Ridge Lakota reservation a few years ago. On this occasion, an elder was giving an opening prayer. His words were made much more important because he used sign language to emphasize a particular point. When he used his hands, not only did he hold our attention with his words, but watching his hand movements was almost like watching a dance.

Today one of the places you still see sign language to a great degree is among the Pueblo people of the Southwest. In many of their public dances, the elders once again are the ones who can be seen speaking with their hands. As the long line of dancers moves up and down the plaza, the elders dance alongside, using their hands to tell the story of how the seeds are planted, how the rains will come to water the plants, and how the plants will grow.

Sign language is an old language, one that was once important for our peoples' survival. Today spoken language is more often used, but the language of silence is still a very important part of our Native American culture and tradition and will most likely remain so for many years to come.

I hope that you enjoy reading this book and that you have fun learning to communicate using sign language.

Louis Mofsie
of the Hopi and Winnebago Tribes

About Native American Sign Language

The Plains peoples of North America included many different tribes, such as the Cheyenne, the Sioux, the Kiowa, and the Pawnee. Each tribe had its own spoken language, with many words and a complex grammar.

The Plains tribes were largely nomadic, which means they didn't settle in one place for long. Only a few tribes built permanent villages. Most of the others roamed the Plains looking for buffalo, which were their main source of food. In their travels, members of one tribe often encountered members of other tribes. In order for different tribes to communicate, the Plains peoples developed a sign language that was understood by all.

This silent language was also useful within a tribe. During a hunt or a battle, it was sometimes important to remain quiet in order to surprise an animal prey or enemy. Sign language enabled tribe members to communicate signals and commands without talking.

Using This Book

The sign language of the Plains peoples uses hand movements to represent important words or ideas. Many signs seem as if they are pictures drawn with the hands. As you make the signs, you may be able to imagine how they came to be used. For example, the sign for *friend*, in which two fingers are raised together, actually means "two who have grown up together." To make the sign for *cat*, you flatten the tip of your nose so it looks like the flat nose of a cat.

The Plains peoples developed hundreds of signs. The ones included here were chosen because they represent words that might be useful to you today. All of the signs are simple to make. Each sign is described in words and illustrated with a picture. An index at the end of the book can help you find the sign for a particular word.

The book is organized into sections that cover specific topics, such as Family, Food, Time, and Weather. A brief overview of each topic relates it to the lives of the Plains people. On the facing page, pictures and descriptions show you how to make the signs for that topic.

With a little practice, you and your friends will soon be communicating in the silent language of the Plains peoples!

Getting Started

Basic hand positions

Here are the basic hand positions you will use for making signs. Most signs are made with the right hand regardless of whether you are right-handed or left-handed.

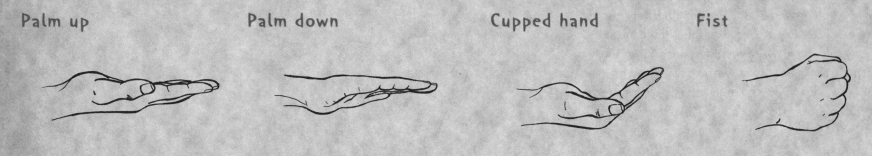

Palm up   Palm down   Cupped hand   Fist

Some useful signs

Here are some simple signs you can use right away! Later, when you've learned the signs in the next chapters, combine them with these to form sentences.

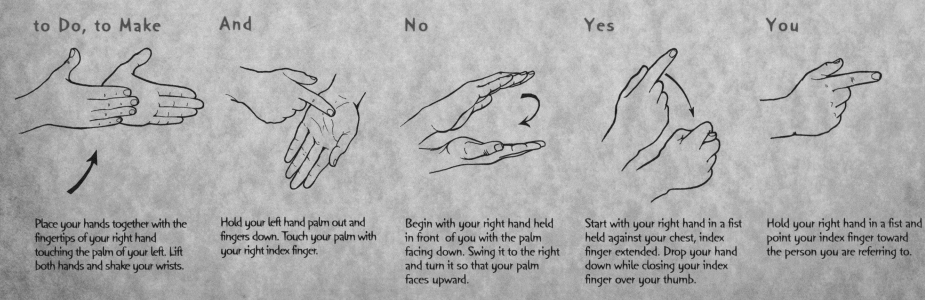

to Do, to Make   And   No   Yes   You

Place your hands together with the fingertips of your right hand touching the palm of your left. Lift both hands and shake your wrists.

Hold your left hand palm out and fingers down. Touch your palm with your right index finger.

Begin with your right hand held in front of you with the palm facing down. Swing it to the right and turn it so that your palm faces upward.

Start with your right hand in a fist held against your chest, index finger extended. Drop your hand down while closing your index finger over your thumb.

Hold your right hand in a fist and point your index finger toward the person you are referring to.

Big

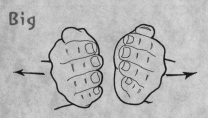

Hold your hands in front of you, palms facing each other but not touching. Spread your hands apart.

Small

Bend your left arm so that your left hand is at shoulder level. With your left hand, hold down the tip of your index finger with your thumb.

Thank you

With hands open and palms down, extend your hands forward. Then lower your hands as far as possible.

Please

With your palm up, hold your right hand against your chest. Slowly move your hand toward the ground.

I, Me, Myself

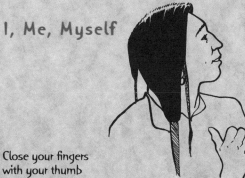

Close your fingers with your thumb pointed toward your chest and point to yourself with your thumb.

Colors

Rub the fingertips of your right hand in a circle on the back of your left hand. Then point to an object that is the same color as the one you want to indicate.

How to ask a question

In order to ask a question, first make this sign, which can mean *what, where, why, when,* or *who,* depending on what follows:

Hold your right hand at the level of your shoulder, palm facing out. Rotate your wrist slightly two or three times.

Possession

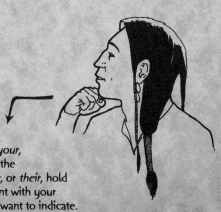

Hold your right fist next to your neck, then bring it forward and down.

To say *my* or *our,* make the possession sign above. To say *your,* make the sign for *you* and then the possession sign. To say *his, her,* or *their,* hold your right hand in a fist and point with your index finger to the persons you want to indicate.

Woman

Use the fingers of your right hand like a comb and stroke downward.

Man

Hold your right index finger up at the level of your chin.

Sister

Make the sign for *woman*. Then touch your lips with your right index and middle fingers and move your hand away from your face.

Brother

Touch your lips with the tips of your right index and middle fingers. Then make the sign for *man*.

Father

Cup your right hand and tap the right side of your chest gently two or three times.

Mother

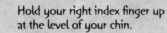

Cup your right hand and tap the left side of your chest gently two or three times.

Baby

Clench your right fist.
Place it against the left side of your chest. With your left hand, grab your right forearm as if you have a baby in your arms.

Sample sentence: Where is my mother?

(question)   (possession)   (mother)

The Family

The family was very important in the lives of the Plains tribes. Among the Sioux, for example, close-knit extended family groups lived and traveled together in search of food. The group was led by an experienced elder leader, and all members worked together in hunting, war, homemaking, and taking care of children and the elderly.

When a baby was born, it was a special occasion for the family. Four days after the baby's birth, a big feast was held, at which time the baby was named. Often, a baby was named after its oldest living grandparent, but sometimes the name of a highly respected grandparent who had already died was used.

Daily Life

The buffalo was essential to the daily life of the Plains peoples. Each tribe had special rituals for hunting these powerful creatures. Even though they killed them, the Plains peoples honored the buffalo and viewed them as brothers who were willing to be sacrificed in order to provide life for the tribe. No part of the buffalo was wasted. The meat was eaten. Hides were used for clothing and shelter. Other parts of the buffalo provided materials for tools, cooking utensils, toys, fuel, weapons, soap, and glue, among other things.

Sample sentence: Hello, my friend.
(hello)   (possession)   (friend)

Day

Begin with both hands flat, palms down, pointed forward. Lift both of your hands at the wrist so the fingers point upward.

Night

Start with both hands flat, palms down, right hand slightly above the left. Move your hands toward each other, crossing the right over the left.

Home

Keeping your hands open, put your fingertips together. Place them against your chest.

Work

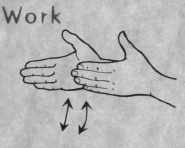

Place hands together pointing forward, the fingertips of your left hand touching the palm of your right hand. Use your wrists to shake your hands up and down slightly several times.

Cat

With your right thumb and index finger, flatten the tip of your nose.

Dog

With your right index and middle fingers extended, pull your hand across your body from left to right.

Friend

Hold your right index and middle fingers up together. Your right arm should be bent at the elbow and your hand at the level of your shoulder. Bring your right hand up to the level of your face, keeping the two fingers raised.

Sleep

Hold both hands, palms together, at the right side of your head. Tilt your head slightly to the right as if you were asleep.

Hello

Hold your right hand up, palm facing forward. Move your hand in a circular motion going toward the right.

to Eat

Cup the fingers of your right hand, fingertips facing your mouth. Move your hand up and down three times.

to Drink

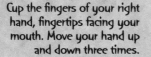

Turn so that your side is facing the other person. Cup your right hand and bring it up slowly to your lips, as if you were drinking. This sign is also used for the word *water*.

Satisfied

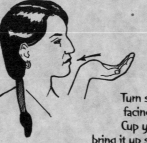

Make a fist with your right hand, your index finger extended. Hold your hand at the level of your stomach, then bring it up to your chin and hold it there for a brief time.

Hungry

With your right palm open, place it in front of your stomach. Move it from side to side several times, as if you were cutting something in half.

to Cook

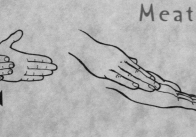

Make the sign for *make* (page 6), then the sign for *eat*.

Meat

Hold your right hand open, palm down, over your left hand, which is open, but palm up. Rub the inside of the left palm with the fingers of your right hand.

Milk

Make both hands into loose fists. Alternately raise and lower your hands, as if you were milking a cow.

Corn

Hold out your left thumb and index finger. Grasp them with your right hand and twist your right hand as if you were shelling corn.

Bread

Place your right open palm across your left open palm, then reverse their positions, left over right, and repeat.

Sample sentence: I am hungry.

(I) (hungry)

Food

For the tribes of the Great Plains, the buffalo was by far the most important source of food—although deer, bear, antelope, wild hens, and turkeys were eaten as well. After a successful buffalo hunt, there was plenty of fresh meat. Some of the meat was dried for use during the winter. The rest was cooked inside a pouch made of buffalo hide that was suspended from four sticks. Hot stones were added to the water in the pouch to make it boil.

Because they were always on the move, a tribe such as the Sioux did not grow its own food. Instead, the women gathered wild cherries, plums, and berries and dug up wild turnips. Fruits and dried vegetables were ground with stones and mixed with dried meat. This mixture, called *pemmican*, was stored in bags or frozen in the winter for future use.

to Write

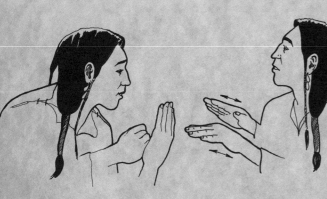

Hold your left hand open with the inside of your hand facing you. Make the motion of holding a pencil in your right thumb and index finger and pretend to write on the left palm.

to Walk

Hold your hands palms down a few inches apart. Drop one hand slightly, pull it back and then push forward, then repeat with the other hand. Do this motion two or three times.

to Talk

Hold your right hand closed near the right side of your mouth. Throw open your fingers two or three times.

to Give

Hold your right hand palm up at shoulder level. Move it forward and down.

to Go

Begin with your right hand flat and facing downward. Swing it to the left as you rotate your palm upward.

to Keep

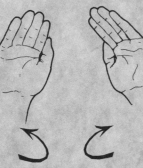

Make a fist with your left hand, keeping the left index finger pointed upward. Grasp the left finger with your right hand and move both hands from right to left.

to Play

Hold up both hands, slightly curved and facing each other. Twist them so that the palms face front and then back several times.

Sample sentence: I am writing to my sister.

(I) (write) (possession) (sister)

(woman)

Actions

The lives of the Plains peoples demanded a lot of hard work, including gathering food, moving camp, hunting, and fighting wars. Tribes were frequently at war with each other, competing for the available buffalo or for horses.

But the Plains peoples also enjoyed their leisure time. Children played games with balls and played make-believe—acting out hunts and battles and setting up house in small tepees. Adults enjoyed guessing games using pieces of bone and gambling games using the pits of plums. Horse races and hoop-and-pole games were other favorite pastimes. When the rivers froze in the winter, adults and children went ice-sledding and played games on the ice, including a game similar to lacrosse.

Time

The Plains tribes estimated days by sleeps, or nights. In order to count months, they counted moons. Years were counted by the number of winters passed.

The Sioux were very interested in recording the passage of time. Certain people in the tribe had the responsibility of keeping the records, called winter counts. Records were painted on deerskin and took the form of pictures that illustrated events. Each year was not labeled with numbers, but was named for the most important event that occurred in that year. For example, a year in which there was an eclipse of the sun might be named The Winter the Sun Died.

Sample sentence: Is it time to go home?

| (question) | (time) | (to go) | (home) |

Now

Hold your right hand out in front of your face in a fist, with your index finger pointing straight up. Move your hand slightly forward and then back to the original position.

Forever

With your open right hand near your right ear, move your hand forward and backward twice.

Future

Make the sign for *time*, then bring your right hand forward with the index finger still extended. Move it over your left hand.

Time

Hold both hands at chest level, index fingers pointing forward, with the remaining fingers closed in fists. Pull your right hand back and to the right about 8 inches (20 cm).

Past

Hold out your left hand. Quickly slide your right hand against it, brushing downward.

Before

Hold both hands in front of you in fists, index fingers pointing forward. Make the sign for *time*. Then push your right hand forward and back.

After

Hold your left hand up, palm open. With your right index finger, draw a line from your palm to your wrist.

Near

Hold your right hand up, curved, palm facing your right shoulder. Pull your hand in toward your shoulder.

Far

Hold your right hand up, curved, palm facing your right shoulder. Bring your hand down in front of you.

Above

Hold both hands flat, right palm down, left palm up, fingers pointing in opposite directions, with your right hand resting on the top of your left hand. Then raise your right hand up a few inches.

Below

Hold both hands flat, palms down, fingers pointing in opposite directions, with your left hand resting on the top of your right hand. Drop your right hand down a few inches.

Up

Use your right index finger to point to the sky.

Down

Use your right index finger to point to the ground.

Across

Hold your left hand out flat, palm down. Cup your right hand and cross it over your left hand.

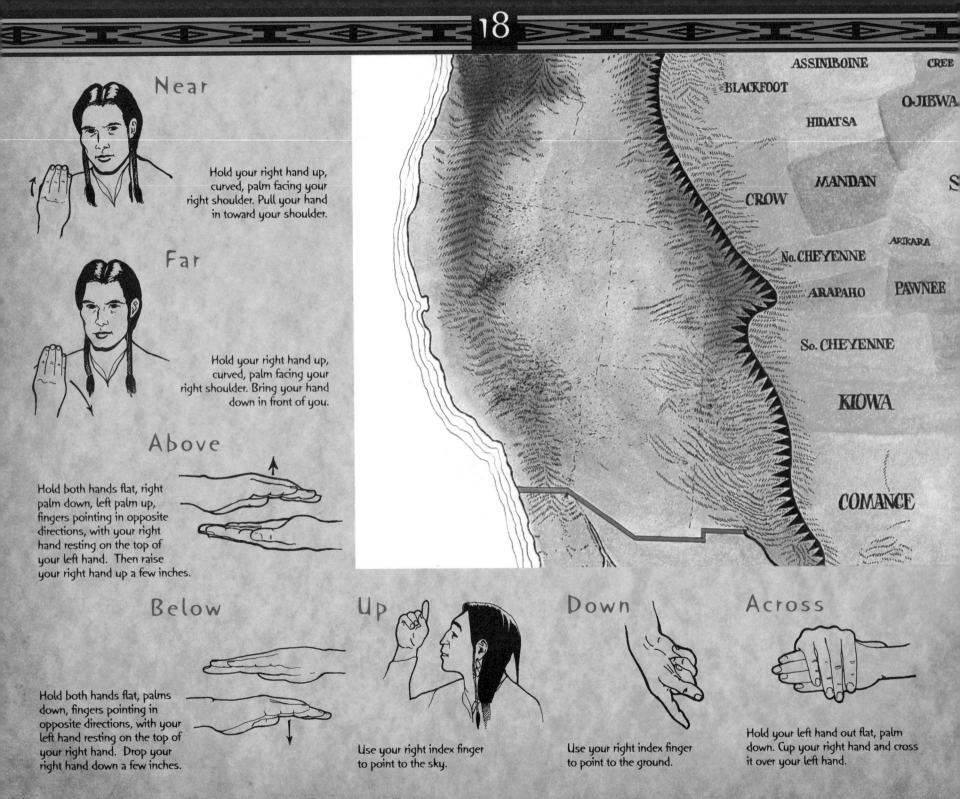

ASSINIBOINE   CREE

BLACKFOOT

OJIBWA

HIDATSA

MANDAN

CROW

ARIKARA

No. CHEYENNE

ARAPAHO   PAWNEE

So. CHEYENNE

KIOWA

COMANCHE

NCA
OTO

OSAGE

EASTERN

HITA

1800-1850

Sample sentence: Your home is far.

(you)	(possession)	(home)	(far)

Getting Places

The tribes of the Plains lived in the areas that are now the states of Montana, Wyoming, Colorado, New Mexico, Texas, Oklahoma, Kansas, Nebraska, South Dakota, North Dakota, Minnesota, Iowa, Missouri, Arkansas, and Louisiana.

Life on the Plains was one of change and movement. Except during the winter, when families or small groups of families settled down to protect themselves from the cold weather, most Plains tribes stayed on the move. If they sighted buffalo, they had to pack up and follow swiftly. In order to ensure quick movement, everything a person owned could be carried by a person, a dog, or a horse.

Earth

Begin with both hands flat in front of your body, palms down. Push your hands downward and away from each other.

Grass

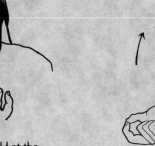

With your hands held at the level of your waist, point fingers upward, keeping them separated. Slowly raise your hands up.

Flower

Make the sign for *grass*. Then make circles with your thumbs and index fingers.

Tree

Hold your left hand about four inches in front of your chest, palm facing inward and fingers spread apart. Shake your hand slightly.

Leaf

Make the sign for *tree*. With your right hand, make a form like a letter c, using your thumb and index finger.

Sun

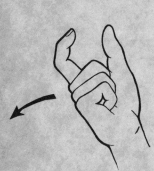

Use the index finger and thumb of your right hand to form an incomplete circle. Move your hand in a curve from left to right.

Moon

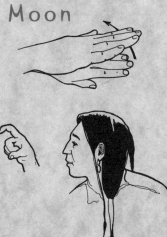

Make the sign for *night* (page 11). Then make the letter c with your right thumb and index finger and lift it up and away from your body.

Sample sentence: The grass is green.

(grass)   (color: green)

Nature

The Plains peoples were very much at home in nature. For instance, they used natural objects they found to help them communicate with one another. The best example of this is in the trail signs they created. Rocks and bones piled up in certain ways might tell someone the direction that should be followed or stand as a warning about dangers that lay ahead. Branches stuck in the soil in different arrangements were used to indicate distances or the number of days it would take to walk to a destination.

Weather

Because they lived close to nature and had to adapt to changes in weather conditions, the Plains tribes had great respect for the natural cycles of the seasons, and they honored them with ceremonies.

The Sun Dance was the most important event of the year for the Plains peoples. Often it was held to celebrate the coming together of the tribe after the winter. For some tribes, the Sun Dance was held in summer in anticipation of the fall buffalo hunt. The ceremony included not only dancing but singing and feasting, as well.

Sample sentence: Is it raining?
(question)   (rain)

Rain

Hold your hands in fists high above your head. Lower them slowly several times, opening your fingers as you bring your hands down.

Snow

Cup your hands, fingers out. Slowly lower them, making curving and zigzag patterns as you lower them.

Wind

Hold your hands side by side, palms down, fingers together. Move your hands forward, shaking them to show the blowing of the wind.

Clouds

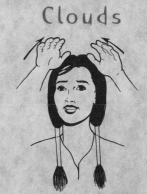

Hold both hands over your head, palms down. Slowly move them upward.

Winter

With your elbows bent, hold both hands in fists, fingers curled in toward your body. Shake your fists as though you are shivering.

Spring

Make the sign for *grass* (page 20), then the sign for *small* (page 7).

Summer

Using two hands, make the sign for *grass* (page 20), raising the hands very high.

Fall

Make the sign for *leaf* (page 20) but hold your left hand still. Bring your right hand down to your waist in a wavy motion.

Love

Make the sign for *friend* (page 11).

Shy

Hold both hands up, palms inward, hands touching either side of your face. Then cross your hands across your face.

Angry

Make a fist with your right hand and place it at the middle of your forehead, with thumb touching forehead. Make twisting motions with your fist.

Afraid

Make two fists, with your fingers facing forward. Extend both index fingers and hook them downward. Pull both arms back.

Sad

Make a fist with your right hand and press it against your forehead, turning your head to one side. Make a small circle with your fist.

Surprised

Put the fingers of your left hand over your mouth and extend your right hand, palm facing outward.

Sample sentence: My brother was surprised.

(possession)   (brother)   (past)   (surprised)

(man)

Feelings and Emotions

Plains peoples had many opportunities for self-expression. They decorated their clothing, tepees, and shields with drawings and designs. Some scholars believe that geometric designs were used to express feelings and emotions. Storytelling was another important way that members of the Plains tribes expressed themselves.

The tribes' elders shared the history of the tribe as well as tales of their own exploits in war. Young children were expected to show respect for their elders by listening carefully to them. Children were not supposed to express their opinions to adults. Adults showed respect for their children as well. Both parents took an active interest in raising their children according to the ways of the tribe.

Hat

Hold your right hand flat above your head. Then bring your hand down in front of you and rest your index finger and thumb against your forehead.

Blanket

Hold both hands in fists, palms facing in, pulled up to your shoulders. Then cross your arms at the wrists, right arm closer to your body.

Bag

Hold your left hand as if it were the opening of a bag, then cup your right hand and put it into the opening.

Book

Hold your hands side by side in front of you, palms up, as if you were reading a book.

Boat

Hold your hands cupped together and move them forward.

Money

Make an incomplete circle with your right thumb and index finger. Curl your other three fingers into a fist. Hold your right hand halfway up your chest.

Clothes

Place the palms of both hands on your chest, then brush them down toward your waist.

Sample sentence: The blanket is red and blue.

(blanket)   (color: red)   (and)   (color: blue)

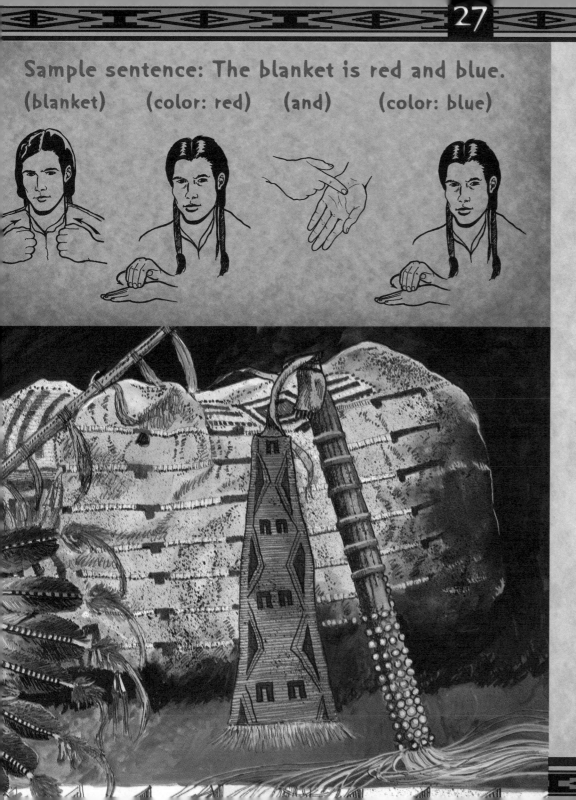

Objects

Because many of the Plains tribes were nomadic, most of their possessions were easily carried items necessary for daily life. Unlike other Native Americans, they did not create much decorative pottery that might be broken when transported.

Some of the objects that were important for everyday use were beautifully decorated. Tepees were often brightly painted with pictures. Women decorated pouches and cases for carrying medicine with porcupine quills and beads sewn into colorful triangle and diamond patterns. Men often painted their buffalo robes with scenes that showed their successes in battle.

Counting and Quantities

Some of the various Plains tribes traded with one another. For example, the Pawnees gave pipestone and eagles' feathers to the Wichitas, the Arkansas, and the Mandans in exchange for horses. The Sioux provided horses, guns, and furs to the Arkansas. Unlike the nomadic Sioux, the Arkansas settled in one area and raised fruits and vegetables, which they traded to the Sioux. However, because there was a lot of fighting among the tribes of the Great Plains, trading was limited.

Sample sentence: I gave half to my friend.

(I)   (past)   (give)   (half)   (possession)   (friend)

Numbers

To indicate numbers from *one* to *five*, close your right hand into a fist with your palm facing away from you. To show *one*, raise your pinky finger. To show *two*, add the ring finger; for *three*, add the middle finger; for *four*, add the index finger; and for *five*, raise all five fingers.

In order to show the numbers *six* through *ten*, keep your right hand as it was for *five*, and make your left hand into a fist. For *six*, raise your left thumb and have it touch your right thumb. For *seven*, raise your left index finger; for *eight*, add your middle finger; for *nine*, add your left ring finger; and for *ten*, raise the pinky on your left hand so that all of your ten fingers are raised.

Half

Hold your left hand flat and pointing to the right. Place your right hand on top of it, flat and open, with fingers pointing straight out toward the person you are addressing. Slide your right hand to the right.

Exchange, Trade

Hold up both hands in fists, with index fingers pointing up. Keeping your index fingers pointed, cross your fingers left in front of right.

All

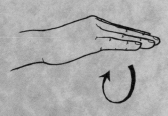

With your right hand held flat, palm down, make a circle from right to left.

All gone

Hold your palms together, right hand on top of left, fingers facing in opposite directions. Brush your right hand across your left palm, sweeping outward.

Much, Many

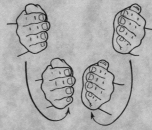

Hold your hands apart, fingers curved, palms facing each other. In a curving motion, move hands downward and then back up so they are nearly touching.

Equal

Hold your hands in fists, index fingers pointing out, and move both hands forward.

Good

Hold your right hand, palm down, against the left side of your chest. Swing your hand upward away from your chest.

Bad

Hold your right fist against the left side of your chest. Opening your fist, make a downward motion toward your right side.

Strong

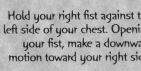

Make both hands into fists and place your right fist on top of your left. Make a twisting motion, as if you were trying to break something.

Brave

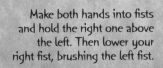

Make both hands into fists and hold the right one above the left. Then lower your right fist, brushing the left fist.

Honest

Hold your right hand in front of your chin, index finger extended away from you and other fingers closed in a fist.

Innocent

Raise both hands, palms open and facing down, to shoulder level. Turn palms toward the other person.

Qualities and Values

The daily life of the Plains peoples was difficult. In facing challenges, they were expected to react and behave according to particular tribal standards and values.

Members of the Plains tribes strove to be brave, wise, and truthful. In addition, they tried to achieve fortitude—mental and emotional strength—while facing danger or pain. Even small children were encouraged to display these qualities.

The Plains tribes recognized the importance of children for passing down their ways of life from generation to generation. For this reason, raising children was among the highest achievements. The value placed on children helped the Plains peoples to survive into the present day.

Sample sentence: My father is strong.

(possession)   (father)   (strong)

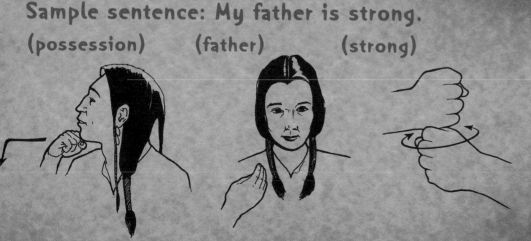

Index